DEDICATION:

TO MOM FOR LIGHTING THE FIRE
AND
DAD FOR POURING GASOLINE ON IT.
.....BRIAN PULIDO

TO MY SON, CHANCE (KID CHAOS).
.....STEVEN HUGHES

CHAPTER
ONE

1

CREATOR/WRITER
BRIAN PULIDO

ARTIST
STEVEN HUGHES

LETTERER
RONALD CRUZ

ERNIE!

ERNIE ERNIE, ERNIE. RISE AND SHINE♪

I TRUST YOU HAD *PLEASANT* DREAMS?

"EVIL" ERNIE FAIRCHILD'S REALITY:

I'M CONCERNED WITH THE CORE OF THE PROBLEM— THE PSYCHOPATH'S KILLING URGE. REMOVE IT AND YOU HAVE A CITIZEN READY FOR SOCIALIZATION.

OUR PRESENT TASK IS A SEARCH FOR A SUITABLE SUBJECT.

REMARKABLE.

VERY REMARKABLE.

LET'S HEAR MORE, *MARY*. TOMORROW.

HEY JUDY I *LOVE* PSYCHO STORIES!

BILLY, I HEAR HE MAKES *CHARLES MANSON* LOOK LIKE A *CHOIRBOY!*

HIS NAME IS *ERNIE FAIRCHILD.*

THESE PANCAKES BEAUTIFUL OR WHAT?

O.K. I'M NO JULIA CHILD. SUE ME!

HEY, HE'S AN UGLY ONE

RICK, YOU ALMOST SCARED ME TO DEATH!

HE'S A PRODUCT OF DEPRAVED, ABUSIVE PARENTS.

MARY, CAN YOU MAKE US A REAL BREAKFAST?

SORRY. I'VE GOT TO GO SEE ERNIE.

9

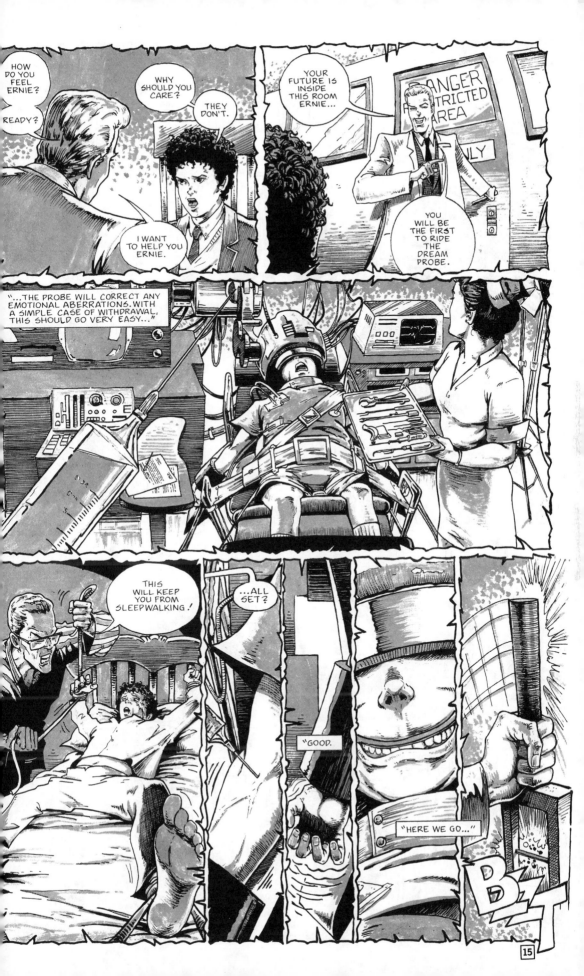

CHAPTER
TWO

EVIL ERNIE'S FANTASY:

SOMETIMES I **WORRY** ABOUT YOU, EVIL ERNIE...

YOU THINK **SMALL**. A MURDER HERE. A MURDER THERE.

WHAT WOULD YOU DO IF YOU HAD **GREAT POWER**?

THE CURE THAT KILLS

CREATED AND WRITTEN BY:	PENCILLED AND INKED BY:	LETTERED BY:
BRIAN PULIDO	STEVEN HUGHES	RONALD CRUZ

5

8

YOU FOOLS!

GET OFF.!

UGH.!

WHAK

GET BEHIND HIM.!

GET THE GUN.!

OUCH.!

STOP HIM.!

KISS IT GOODBYE, ERNESTO.!

WHOOP!

UGH.! ...YOU THINK *THAT'LL* STOP ME?!

YOU'RE DREAMIN'. IT'LL TAKE MORE'N THAT...

I'LL...

...SEE...

...YOU...

...IN...

...HELL...

WHAT A BLAST! CREEP GOT *EXACTLY* WHAT HE DESERVED.

COULDN'T HAVE HAPPENED TO A *NICER* GUY.

...WE HAVE A BODY.

CAN YOU PICK IT UP, PRONTO?

GREAT.

I'M SERIOUS. ERNIE IS DEAD.

I'M SORRY.

SORRY?!

MY *REPUTATION* IS ON THE LINE!

WE'RE HAVING OFFICIALS OVER HERE TO *CELEBRATE* YOUR SUCCESS, DAMN IT!

THEY *FUNDED* NEUROTECH.

AS FAR AS I'M CONCERNED, IT WAS A *SUCCESS!* AND YOU BETTER GO ALONG WITH ME MARY.

NOW GET *OVER* HERE!

I'M LEAVING. I'LL CHECK IN LATER.

CHAPTER THREE

GREAT!

I *QUIT* WORKING HERE 'CAUSE THAT ERNIE KID *SPOOKED* ME, NOW I GOTTA COME *BACK.*

WHO AM I PICKIN' UP ANYWAY?

ERNIE FAIRCHILD!

HA! CREEP KICKED THE BUCKET.

WHAT DID DR. PRICE CALL HIM?

THE DOMINO KILLER–HE'D KILL *ANYTHING* HE LAID HIS HANDS ON.

TOO FREAKY.

THEY WERE *SUPPOSED* TO *CURE* HIM TODAY. GUESS THE TREATMENT *BACKFIRED.*

SERVES HIM RIGHT.

HE WAS NOTHING BUT A *PUNK* ANYWAY.

KEYS PLEASE!

EVIL ERNIE!

YOU'VE... *CHANGED!*

YOU WANT THE KEYS? NO PROBLEM. GIMME A SECOND.

ANYTHING YOU SAY, ERNIE!

MURDER MARDI GRAS

IN SUBURBIA

TIME'S UP!

GO!

A-150

CREATED AND WRITTEN BY // PENCILLED AND INKED BY // LETTERED BY
BRIAN PULIDO // **STEVEN HUGHES** // **RONALD CRUZ**

14

CHAPTER FOUR

4

THE MAN AND WOMAN IN THE MIDDLE ARE HIS PSYCHO-THERAPISTS. THEIR TAMPERING CREATED *EVIL ERNIE.*

GOT IT!

COOL IT.

THE SITUATION'S UNDER CONTROL.

TAKE *THAT*, BEEFARONI FACE!

UUUUGHH...

ELSEWHERE...

MASS HYSTERIA? GENERAL, WHATEVER YOU CALL IT, HALF MY TOWN IS REPORTING ATTACKS.

YES, YES, WE'LL BE OUT THERE. WE'RE GETTIN' OUR ORDERS NOW, HONEY.

WHAT DO WE *DO*?

YOU BETTER HURRY UP AN' GET HERE!

WE GOTTA DO *SOMETHIN'*! THEY'RE *DYIN'* OUT THERE!

I TALKED TO THE ARMY. OUR ORDERS ARE TO ESTABLISH A BARRICADE ON TURTLE LAKE BRIDGE AND STOP *ANYTHING* THAT CROSSES.

TURTLE LAKE BRIDGE...

HHAHA HAAAAAA!

GET IT IN THE **HEAD!**

SUBURBIA.

THOUGH THE BULLET ONLY GRAZES EVIL ERNIE'S HEAD, THE GHOULS FEEL ITS AGONIZING EFFECTS ON THEIR MASTER.

ERNIE'S PAIN IS THEIR PAIN.

BUT THE PAIN SUBSIDES...

HIT IT IN THE HEAD AGAIN! IT DIDN'T LIKE THAT!!

...AND IN SUBURBIA, THE **MURDER MARDI GRAS** CONTINUES.

INSIDE DR. MARY YOUNG'S HOME...

WE NEVER SHOULD HAVE TRUSTED STONE. THAT AMBITIOUS *FOOL!* WE'RE *RUINED!*

"A MENTAL PURIFICATION DEVICE." WHAT WERE WE *THINKING??*

GOD FORBID IT GETS OUT THAT YOU *APPROVED* THIS TEST!

YOU CAN KISS YOUR MERCEDES GOOD-BYE, AM I RIGHT?

ABSOLUTELY.

I SUGGEST DR. MARY YOUNG IS AT FAULT.

HER MACHINERY DID THE DEED.

I *LIKE* IT.

THEN IT'S SETTLED. DR. YOUNG TAKES THE BLAME.

YOU THINK I DIDN'T *HEAR* THAT? WHY DID MARY GET INVOLVED WITH YOU MANIPULATIVE BASTARDS?

WE DON'T EVEN KNOW IF SHE'S *ALIVE!*

WE SHOULD THROW YOU *OUT* WITH THOSE THINGS!

RIGHTEOUS IDEA!

I'M TEMPTED.

15

LADY DEATH?

INSIDE EVIL ERNIE'S MIND IS A NIGHTMARE NETHERWORLD OF HIS OWN MAKING WHERE ALL IS DEAD OR DYING. IT IS HIS SANCTUARY, THIS EVIL PLACE.

IT IS HIS FANTASY.

LADY DEATH!

FIND ME,
AND I'M
YOURS.

HUH?

IDEALISM.

THE DISEASE OF *IDIOTS*.

LINE'S DEAD.

I WONDER HOW BILLY, JUDY AND RICK ARE HOLDING UP.

PLEASE LET THEM BE ALL RIGHT.

IT WASN'T SUPPOSED TO TURN OUT THIS WAY.

I ONLY WANTED TO HELP.

I *HAVE* TO REACH MY FAMILY!

GOOD LORD, WHAT HAVE WE *CREATED*?

DAMN!

BLAM

CHAPTER
FIVE

I DID IT! I KILLED EVIL ERNIE!

IN SUBURBIA...

ERNIE'S PAIN IS **THEIR** PAIN!

ERNIE'S ARMY OF THE UNDEAD **WRITHE** IN AGONY!

GRRRRRR

GRRRR

IMPOSSIBLE!

NOT!

4

5

INSIDE EVILERNIE'S MIND...

NO!

THIS IS NO TIME FOR *POINTLESS DIVERSIONS!* THERE ARE TOO MANY *LIVING* LEFT! WE HAVE A *DEAL*, ERNIE!

LISTEN TO ME!!

STUPID LITTLE BOY. THIS WILL BE YOUR *UNDOING*.

ENOUGH!

I'VE HAD *ENOUGH!!*

SUCK ON THIS!

NO WAY THAT *CREEP'S* GONNA GET *MY* FAMILY!

6

LISTEN—GO TO THE ROOF AND *HIDE*. DON'T COME DOWN, NO MATTER *WHAT*.

FORGET IT, MAN. WE'RE *STAYIN'.*

WE'LL *FIGHT*.

WE CAN'T TELL *WHO'S* COMING. IF IT'S MORE GHOULS, I SAY WE SACRIFICE THE *KIDS*.

GOO CAL STON

YOU GUTLESS *DWEEB!* DON'T EVEN *THINK* OF IT!

IF *ANYBODY* GOES, IT'S *YOU*, STONE!

CAN'T THIS CRATE GO ANY *FASTER*?

LOOK, I DON'T KNOW HOW TO *OPERATE* THAT THING BACK THERE. YOU BETTER CLAM UP AND KEEP READIN' THAT *MANUAL!*

WHAT THE HELL IS GOING *ON* OUT THERE?!

CAN'T SEE A *THING!*

15

QUICK! THIS WAY, BILLY!

YUCK!

ERNIE?

YESSSS... THE FAMILY!!

18

CASE CLOSED.

MARY! YOU DID IT!

THE GHOULS ARE DEAD!

WHERE'S ERNIE?

I CURED HIM!

YOUR SIST REALLY PA A WALLO LET ME T YOU.

GOOD W MAR

VICE VERSA.

INSIDE THE HOUSE...

—WE ON? OKAY, GOOD MORNING, LADIES AND GENTLEMEN. AS SUDDENLY AS IT STARTED, THE MYSTERIOUS *PSYCHO PLAGUE* HAS *ENDED*.

LOSS OF LIFE IS IN THE THOUSANDS, PERHAPS *TENS* OF THOUSANDS, AND DAMAGES APPROACH MULTI-*BILLION* DOLLAR FIGURES...

WHAT'S THAT?

OUCH!

STONE!

23

THE END.

Steven Hughes
Sketchbook

CHAOS! ARCHIVES

ON THE FOLLOWING PAGES YOU
WILL FIND THUMBNAIL SKETCHES
FOR EVIL ERNIE #1 WHICH
FEATURE A DIFFERENT "DREAM PROBE"
SEQUENCE & A DIFFERENT
INTRODUCTION FOR LADY DEATH.

SNUFF SAID!

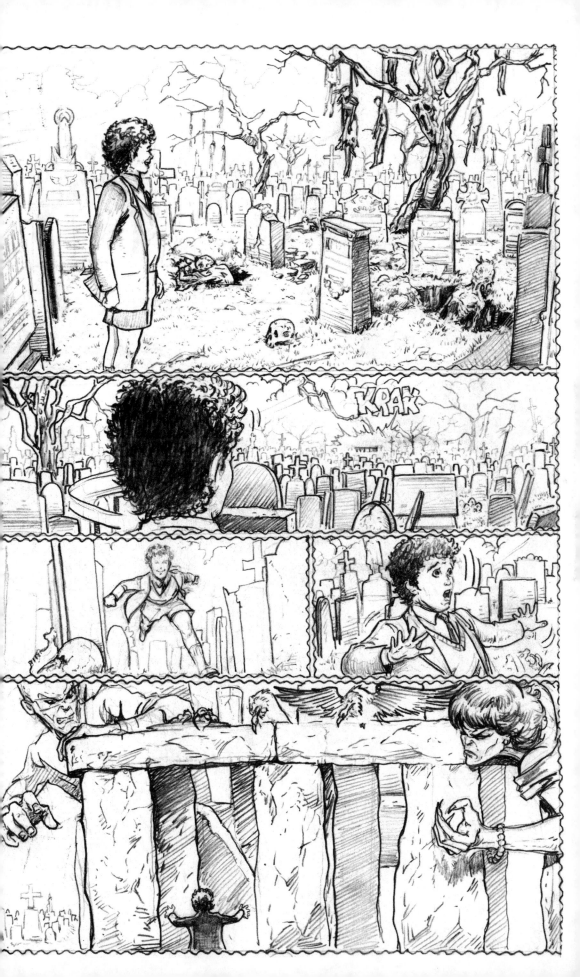